POTENTIALS IN THE GRAVE YARD

An Indication of Purposeless Life

JONAH SUNDAY MORENIKEJI

SUNKEM PUBLISHING INT'L

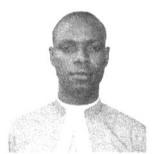

Copyright © 2020 JONAH SUNDAY MORENIKEJI

All rights reserved

No part of this book may be reproduced, or stored in a retrieval system, or transmitted in any form or by any means, electronic, mechanical, photocopying, recording, or otherwise, without express written permission of the publisher.

ISBN: 9798738373121

Cover design by: SUNKEM PUBLISHING INT'L
Contact Number: 08101845185
sundaymorenikeji4@gmail.com

I dedicate this book to God Almighty, the fountain and giver of inspiration for the fulfillment of this project. All Glory to Him for the wisdom and strength to write this book.

CONTENTS

Title Page	1
Copyright	2
Dedication	3
Foreword	7
Introduction	11
Preface	15
Prologue	17
CHAPTER 1- I. THE WORD POTENTIAL	27
	31
II. THE PLACE CALLED GRAVEYARD	
	34
III. THE IMPORTANCE OF POTENTIAL IN LIFE	
CHAPTER 2- IDENTIFYING AND DISCOVERING YOUR PURPOSE WITHIN THE SCOPE OF YOUR POTENTIAL	38
I. Pay Attention to your Imaginatios	43
II. Pay Attention to Things You Love To Do	46
	48
III. Pay Attention to What People Say About You	
CHAPTER 3- REALIZING POTENTIAL IN YOU AND CHANNEL IT TOWARDS ITS PURPOSE	51
	53

I. Confirm Your Potentials

55

II. Get Yourself Ready

58

III. Set Goals For Yourself

CHAPTER 4-   FULFILLING YOUR PURPOSE WHILE YOU ARE LIVING.   68

69

I. COMMITTED TO YOUR FULL POTENTIAL

74

II. FIGHT AGAINST DISTRACTION AROUND YOU

III. Unleash Your Potential   89

Avoid A Purposeless Life   95

Chapter 5-   POTENTIALS IN THE GRAVEYARD   98

107

Procrastination: An Enemy Of Potential

Danger of Unused Potential   112

Do not be unfruitful   114

117

Live to Your Full Potential

Acknowledgement   123

About The Author   127

Untitled   129

131

Afterword   131

FOREWORD

The book, Potentials in the Graveyard is a book written by Rev'd Morenikeji Jonah Sunday. It is a book written to remind the young and old that there is potential(s) in every living soul. This potential(s) should be put in use while alive, not to be abandoned, disregarded, and buried.

The author in his conviction tried to direct every man and woman to the means of identifying the potential(s) in oneself. Another way of understanding the potential(s) in man is the gifts or talents according to the author. The gifts in man when properly utilized give him an identity, make him relevant and useful to his generation. The potential(s) in man should be developed. The author did well to have given methods of development and actualization. In his discovery, many people do not know the purpose of their life or existence. To such people, their potential(s) remain in them, sleep in them, and die with them unused. What a waste!

"Potentials in the Graveyard" is a book written under the inspiration of God as a result of some observation made of how most people live a purposeless life. The book in your hands will help you to discover yours and give you directions on how to put them to work early in life because the days when you won't be able to do them are close by. It is on this bases, everybody will give an account of his life to God at the end of life.

I feel delighted to recommend the book to every good thinking person, but more especially to young ones, students, and all those who want to be relevant in this world. The book is good for even counselors and career developers to guide people.

The Rt. Rev'd Tasie, Ikemefule K. JP

Bishop, Diocese of Ngbo.

Methodist Church Nigeria

INTRODUCTION

The world is full of different mineral resources that are yet to be discovered. The information on air cannot be exhausted, especially on microwave signals or frequency. Almost every needed resource for the accomplishment of a purposeful life is available at human disposal. In the creation story according to the Scripture God created everything perfectly before the existence of human beings and God created man as the manager of other things created. Everything that man needs to function in existence and fulfillment of the purposes in the world is embedded in the creation. However, it is left for the man to discover these things and make use of them for the glory of God.

It is cleared that nothing exists in this world without purpose for its existence, whether discovered or not discovered nothing exists by accident.

I discovered that human nature is full of different kinds of gifts, talents, and the ability to fulfill a divine assignment. This trait is called potentials. This is an inborn ability in every man because he is created with it. This makes one man different and unique from others when articulated, actualized, and utilized well.

My discovery has shown that many people in

this life had wasted and are wasting their potential without realizing and utilizing it for their purpose of existence in life, with that, many died with it and were buried in the graveyard with it. What a great loss!

The undiscovered and unutilized potential is a waste and useless to humanity which the original owner or giver (God) will not be happy with the person that lived a purposeless life and wasted his or her potential (ability to create)

This book will help in knowing what potential is all about, its importance, and reveal how to realize and utilize one's potential for existence.

PREFACE

Potential is ability in you that exists in passive, not active, which is capable of being active and utilizing to discover and fulfill your purpose of existence.

They are abilities and capacities that man is endowed with by the Creator to create things in this world without man being aware of them. In this book, I call it potential. This potential does not just exist in man for existing sake; there is a purpose for its existence in man.

However, my observation in life baffles me so much, when I see many people die and bury without releasing their potential for the fulfillment of their purpose in life, whereas potential is not to be dormant in the graveyard, but to be realized and utilized

This was what triggers me some months ago to produce a tract on this topic "potential in the graveyard" but my experience with Flourish Joshua writers and speakers Academy, where I was groomed in writing and speaking made it elaborate to this point.

This book will give more details.

Morenikeji, Jonah Sunday

June 2020

PROLOGUE

EXCERPT

The graveyard is said to be the richest place on the planet earth. It contains the books unwritten, inventions not made, sermons not preached, songs not sung and many lives not lived. An unused brain is valued to be the most expensive. This is because we already know the extent to which the used ones like that of Albert Einstein could go and how much it could achieve but the power locked up in a crude brain cannot be underestimated. Fallow land is known to be the most fertile farmland. No man has tapped from it for a very long time and it's ready to give it's best to seeds if given the opportunity. The unactualized potentials are by far the greatest forces on earth. The earth is waiting for the full manifestation of these gifts of God in man to change situations around and deliver it from the impending crisis hanging over it and make it a better place to live in.

Potential is a silent, passive, and gentle guest locked up inside of men waiting to be introduced. It all starts with a step and I believe reading this book is one of the big steps needed in the pursuit of purpose and maximizing your potential. Myles Munroe said, "if a man fulfills his full potentials before departing this world, he dies but when he couldn't fulfill his God-deposited potentials, such a man is killed". That means we have not lived until we fulfill the volume of the book that is written about us by our Maker (God).

It is the passion of the author that the graveyard would no longer rob the earth of its best resources and that no other potential will be buried in the black hole. The book was birth with a purpose, that all men will discover, actualize, and utilize their God-given potentials. This book opens up the readers to precise and practicable instructions as well as nuggets that will equip the reader with the right ammunitions needed to navigate the web of realizing and unleashing their potentials. I love the fact that the author did not stop at propelling or motivating but also offers solutions and suggestions on how potentials can be discovered and fulfilled on earth. Happy Reading.

Pastor Ife Adetona

President, Sons, and Daughters of Zion Worldwide

EXCERPT

An accomplished and prolific writer Rick Warren in his book "The Purpose-driven Life" says,

"You are not an accident. Your birth was not a mistake or mishap, and your life is no fluke of nature. Your parents may not have planned you, but God did. He was not at all surprised by your birth, He expected it. Long before you were conceived by your parents, you were conceived in the mind of God. He thought of you first. It is not fate, nor luck, no coincidence that you are breathing at this very moment. You are alive because God created you to fit into His plan for humanity."

The writer of the book of Jeremiah quoting God's message to Jeremiah says; "Before I formed you in the womb, I knew you, before you were born, I set you apart; I appointed you as a prophet to the nations". Jer. 1:5.

No one on earth was created without a purpose or to make up the number of a certain race or people. Every man was uniquely created to fulfill a certain purpose God intended for him. The writer of the book of Psalm says "I praise thee, for I am fearfully and wonderfully made. Your works are wonderful I know that full well". Psalm 139:14.

Every man is created with a destiny to fulfill. This is what the author term "Potential". This potential cannot be gotten from education or any other human source or resource. Everyone was created with it and no man/woman was ever created without it.

The pertinent questions now are; Why is the greater percentage of the dead buried with these potentials? How can the living unlock theirs to employ them to the glory of their maker(GOD), and the benefit of men who is the object of that potentials?

The answers to those questions are not far-fetched. Every gadget manufactured has the manufacturer's manual. This manual is the manufacturer's direction for usage. If the user follows/adheres to these directions; the product will attain the purpose of the manufacturer, it will live out its life span and will benefit its user and others to the glory and honor of the manufacturer.

Man is God's highest manufactured gadget, made for his pleasure, which is to serve His purpose. "Thou art worthy, O Lord, to receive glory and power: For thou has created all things and for thy pleasure, they are and were created". Rev. 4:11. The pleasure of God for man is that he attains his full potentials to God's glory and man's benefit. But the reverse is the case to most of the dead. The reason is that they fail to make use of their maker (God's) manual for life and living 'THE BIBLE', but rather turned to men's manual for life and living to their detriment, and as a result, ended their journey on earth without attaining their potentials, and so were buried with them.

The writer of the second letter of peter, says; "His divine power has granted to us all things that pertain to life and Godliness, through the knowledge of Him who called us to his glory and excellence". 2 Peter 1:3. To avoid the mistakes of those dead and buried, without maximizing their potentials is to fall back to our creator's manual of life and living (THE BIBLE) from where we will draw the knowledge of His son Jesus and His plans for us. The writer of 2 Peter 1:3 says; grant us all that pertains to life and Godliness. This will make our lives reflect God's glory and we will, in turn, attain life's excellence to which we were created.

I congratulate Rev. Jonah Sunday Morenikeji

for his wonderful work. This book is food for thought and an eye-opener to the living. It is a must-read to all who wish to avoid the mistake of the dead and those who want to become relevant to their generation.

Very Rev. Elijah E. Okwor

Synod Secretary

Methodist Church of Nigeria

Diocese of Ngbo

CHAPTER 1- I. THE WORD POTENTIAL

The word potential is used in a wide variety of fields. The way it is used in a scientific field is different from the philosophical field, the same way it is used in a gravitational field and electrical field. However, for this book, I will say potential is the latent qualities or ability that may be developed and lead to future success or usefulness. In other words, it is currently an unrealized ability.

Myles Munroe said: *Potential is the sum of whom you are that you have yet to reveal. It is a deposit that waits to be released and maximized. You are capable of much more than you are presently thinking, imaging, doing, or being.*

Your potential is your ability for future ambition

which you must get realized. The prospect and possible aspect of your ability which is yet to be articulated are known as potential. Undeveloped capacity, talent, and aptitude are seen as potential. We can also view potential as anything that is an existing impossibility and capable of developing into actuality. It is dormant power, untapped strength, unused gift, and hidden talent. Potential exists to support the world of ideas and imaginations as conceived in the human mind, ignited by critical thinking and a well-detailed plan. A pregnant woman knows that she is carrying a baby or babies but no one knows the skin color of the child or what the baby will become. This reality is revealed when the child is born.

Likewise, the potential cannot be measured neither will it be understood nor recognized until it is been realized and utilize before it could be recognized in one's life.

Potential is also seen as a capacity for human existence. Since there is no man without potential. It is the major reason you have the assignment you are created for. The enablement and ability which you are created without knowing or being aware of it.

In a lay man's understanding, 'Potential" is not far from you. It is inborn. Sometimes it appears to you in your imagination. This potential is capable of conceivable, generable, thinkable, etc something hypothetic or theoretic and it can also be achievable, attainable, doable, workable, and practicable particularly when working. Trusting in your potential will make you know that YOU can do more than what you are doing have done because it is your strength and capacity to carry out or fulfill your assignment and set goals. Potential is something in you that exists in passive, not active, which is capable of being active when discovered. After being discovered it becomes your identity. Something you are known for among the multitude.

II. THE PLACE CALLED GRAVEYARD

According to the Merriam-Webster dictionary, a graveyard is a piece of land used for burying the Dead. It is also known as cemetery, memorial Park, tomb, sepulcher, burial ground, or Potter's Field.[1] An online English dictionary defines it as" a final storage place for collections of things that are no longer useful or usable"[2]

The place called graveyard with the above descriptions is a place where the living cannot survive. It is a place of abandonment forever. Evan Elsa once said that: "the only place where you can find equality is in the cemetery". Of a truth, the cemetery is not a place of living that moves or claims anything. No one is great and no one is small. It is a silent place that cannot be helped or disturbed by those threw there. The rich, poor, aged, youngest, big, small, fat, and thin were all lying equally. Only the living being who is working there or connected to a deceased (the bereaved ones) that can make a difference from one tomb and other, just for identification of their deceased at the cemetery or graveyard. But for the dead, once they depart, they are equal as far as their strength or power is concerned.

Once anybody or anything goes there, there is no hope of coming back again. It is a place of wastage and destruction. It is also seen as a place of non-existence. It is a place of dormant glory, destiny, and potential. It is any place where the dead are deposited for final resting.

III. THE IMPORTANCE OF POTENTIAL IN LIFE

Life does not exist in a vacuum. Many things in this world appear to be meaningless to man. However, nothing does exist without purpose. In God's agenda, He created everything for at least for a reason or more. Many plantations that some tagged as ordinary grasses are very useful to others that know how to utilize them. There is a very good vegetable leaf in western Nigeria called jute Mallow (its local name in the Western part "Yoruba" is EWEDU: its local name in the Northern part "Hausa" is RAMA, its local name in the Eastern part "Igbo" is AHINGHARA) which is very important in cooking but, in Eastern Nigeria, it is of no value because it appears as ordinary grass. That is to make us understand that everything in this life has its importance and value. Though, it may appear insignificance and valueless to us because we have not tried it but, that does not make it useless.

The importance of potential is not money-making as many people think. The financial or commercialization aspect of ability cannot be overlooked or shunned but, it should not be the priority at the beginning of realizing and releasing potential. Some have a sense of fulfillment when they are educated, employed, married, have kids, purchased vehicles, built houses, and having shares bought in insurance companies as investments. The truth remains that fulfillment and happiness can not be generated from the aforementioned list, there is more to your existence because you are not a mistake!

Life is built on different philosophies which make humans have a different approach to issues. However, the importance of potential does not bring any confusion because it is all about impacting lives and changing your world positively.

Potential in life cannot be overemphasized for its importance, becauseevery human came with a unique potential for the benefits of mankind. The creator of all living souls (GOD) designed everyone with the potential for accomplishing some significant assignments planet earth.

Potential that is harnessed distinguishes you from others around you; it is not for fun. Potential is not to be dormant but to be activated. Your potential is your natural abilities and qualities which are to be engaged and utilized for its importance.

The importance of potential in life is for the growth of humanity. The potential you have is not for selfishness it is rather the benefit of others. Many people discovered their potentials in life but were unable to live to their full capacity and missed the importance of potential which is to adequately affect the world with great purpose. Potential is to be realized, activated, and utilized for the glory of the giver (GOD). When talking about potential and its importance, it is the ability and capacity inherent in you and the tool for impact on planet earth.

CHAPTER 2- IDENTIFYING AND DISCOVERING YOUR PURPOSE WITHIN THE SCOPE OF YOUR POTENTIAL

Mineral resources commonly needed for human daily life does not stay on the surface of the Earth. Some are under rocks, underground and some exist at the lower part of water. These resources can only be discovered and accessed after much effort from the researchers, such as getting a microscope to know exactly where the substance is located; many times it involves the vast knowledge of archaeologists with modern machinery to dig deep into the earth to mine out the mineral.

As mineral resources exist in passive without

any sign of activeness until when a man touches and refines it, so also the manpower in human life is dormant until a man takes a step to activate it. This process of activation is only possible with the help of a supernatural being (God) because the potential in you to do exploit does not exist in a vacuum, you are being endowed by your Creator who made you. If you are not in tune with the living God (your Creator) you are just like somebody who is freely using a product without acknowledging the producer and when the product was faulty he did not know how to reach out to the producer for rebranding. You are a product of a Perfect Designer.

In digging deep to discover the purpose and potentials of your life, you may encounter many things that are beyond the natural eyes of which might demand undergoing spiritual exercise. And of course, the destiny of a man exists in the spiritual than the physical sense before its discovery. This is why some individuals find it difficult to discover purpose. Your purpose in life has a close relationship with the divine (spirituality) because it communicates both realms for the declaration of your fame. Some people by the way of being spiritual in fulfilling their purpose of existence do communicate evil spirits through gods and goddesses which is not the proper means because it is contrary to the will of the originator (God) of destiny.

For easy identification of your purpose within the scope of your potential, you must be conversant with God,The Powerful Being that purposely purposed all the purposes for human existence. The journey of destiny should not be embarked on lightly or nonchalantly if you don't want to fall into the hands of the kingdom of darkness that always cage and kill the destiny in man.

Potential as fueling power in man to fulfill and achieve the divine assignment in man's life, could be a waste or discard if not properly handle maximize. It is agreeable that every human being here on earth has his or her potential to release in life. However, not everybody knows how to go about it, which makes many people died with their potential unused.

This aspect of identification of one's purpose in life is very crucial and important. If anyone will live his or her maximal exploitation of potential in life he or she must begin to search and think about what life is all about at this stage. (Stage of identification). Identifying your purpose through your potential in life is important to your overall happiness and feeling of fulfillment. Discovering what makes you tick is integral to identifying your purpose.

Let us consider the following steps in identifying and realizing a purpose for existence.

I. PAY ATTENTION TO YOUR IMAGINATIOS

Some think that imagination is just for kids, but we all use ours every moment of every day. Imagination is defined as "the act or power of forming a mental image of something not present to the sense of never before wholly perceived in reality". In other words, imagination is the ability to see something with our minds that we cannot see with our physical eyes.

Our imagination is very essential, we cannot do without it. However, it is unfortunate that most of the time we don't listen to ourselves through imagination which is not good enough. There is no how one could identify his or her purpose without listening and paying attention to the imagination. Imagination is the image within us as a human being through which many times will conceive the idea of what we will like to do before actualizing them. If imagination and ideas in one's mind can be properly managed, it will help in quickly identifying one's purpose.

Your imagination also includes your night dreams. If you are finding yourself in dreams doing something meaningful and beautiful to human beings and you always drive joy in it when you wake up, work it out. All the thoughts you are having in you that can make difference in the world, work on them. Identify them for growth.

II. PAY ATTENTION TO THINGS YOU LOVE TO DO

To identify your purpose in life also called for personal and self-examination. The problem is that many people don't pay attention to themselves. When there is no time for reflection on one's life he or she may continue the same way for long without being fulfilled in life.

It is when you calm down and begin to reason with yourself, and then you will need to ask yourself some questions like these. "What am I meant to do in life? How will I discover the purpose of my existence?"

After being overwhelmed with the thought above, you will need to study yourself more and more. Think very well on what you have been doing so far in your life. Is there anything you drive joy in doing? What makes you happy most when you are doing it? Is it your performance in music, writing, teaching, inventing, etc.? Think about things you always do at ease which are very important to humanity. Write them down and identify among them the one you can do better. To identify and discover your purpose is not difficult if you can pay attention to what you love to do on daily basis.

III. PAY ATTENTION TO WHAT PEOPLE SAY ABOUT YOU

Well purpose defined will help to impact people in the world, nevertheless, you need people around to define your purpose sometime and take it to the right channel. An anthropologist can come out with the facts about the customs and behaviors of some people in a particular place as a result of his or her studies. Humans are extremely good at observing one another's character, probably because of relationships.

So, you cannot live in isolation and discover your purpose of living, you must have people around you which in one way or the other say something about what they see in you. Frankly, the fact is that those people at times help you to identify your full potential to fulfill your purpose in life. For instance, sometimes in 2007, I was coming to the house and I met a group of friends in our house discussing, I joined them to make my contribution. Suddenly, a lady spoke aloud! Brother Sunday, you ought to be a Pastor! I was surprised because I had spiritually settled the matter with God before then.

Another one happened when I was addressing the choir as one of the members, a woman just exclaimed that Sunday you supposed to be a teacher because you talk too much with detailed explanation. Though, before this time I have identified my purpose but it has not been acted on.

Nevertheless, you will have your concept of whom you are and what you are good at. Paying attention to what others say about you will offer insight into some of your talents and skills which you might not have considered.

CHAPTER 3- REALIZING POTENTIAL IN YOU AND CHANNEL IT TOWARDS ITS PURPOSE

One thing is to identify your purpose within your capacity another thing is to bring it into existence. Sometimes you may be talking to yourself or someone else that "I know that I have more to offer, but I don't know how to go about it". Failure to bring what you have identified into actualization which is the beginning and the commencement of utilizing your full potential in reality is the same thing as untapped potential. I begin to wonder when I see people using potential on things that are not meaningful and important. It does baffle me a lot when the purpose is being neglected and potential is being utilized but, not for divine assignments. This chapter will help you on how to realize and utilize your potential and channel it toward the purpose which you have confirmed in the previous chapter.

I. CONFIRM YOUR POTENTIALS

The area of confirmation is very important before you start discharging potential. In order not to be confused along the line and crack or stop halfway in the journey of life. Those gifts you have identified as an area of your interest and focus on fulfilling the life purpose will be achieved when you are convinced that you are the potential in fulfilling them. Take, for instance, the student was brilliant in almost all the subjects with better performance in economics while in junior secondary school, when the time comes to study in senior secondary school, he chose to study science instead of accounts. Before he could understand, it was late, and this affected his final result. You must be assured and convinced of what you carry and the trend you can go about it. No students will be given a certificate from any institution except he or she has completed his or her stipulated courses of training in both theory and practical. The student must go to the field to practicalize the training he/she has acquired before he will be awarded a certificate. If you are not sure of yourself about your capacity to launch out your, it may lead to disaster or failure in performance.

II. GET YOURSELF READY

This is another aspect that should not be underestimated at all. Here comes preparation for launching out your potential through good purpose defined. Knowing fully well that potential is an inborn ability with the capacity to birth into reality. Birthing potentials into reality demands lots of effort from you daily. The knowledge of this fact triggers you to learn more about that particular mission. At this point, it is imperative to associate with gifted individuals in the same direction as you. If you are gifted in something, probably you have identified it as your purpose; without getting more knowledge about it, you cannot perform better or birth results.

Therefore, it is also necessary for you to study more on your discoveries and confirm the WHY behind it. This will Foster your wiliness, preparedness, and readiness in releasing your potential outside there for impartation through your purpose. For instance, music as a whole is being studied at the Universities or other tertiary institutions. You are the one to know your area whether to be trained as a professional instrumentalist, vocalist or composer, etc.

There are many areas of studies in schools that can help you prepare enough. Apart from normal or proper school training, there are many certified schools of learning e.g., if you want to be a motivational public speaker and certified writer and author, join some online schools. I can recommend one of the best I know (Flourish Joshua writers and speakers Academy). It is a place to be if you want to become a change agent to your generation.

Whatever you discover about yourself and want to train yourself more on it, you can always find help if you seek them in the right places.

III. SET GOALS FOR YOURSELF

At this point, you must have realized that you have a purpose to fulfill in the world through potential. There must be a proper plan for that. Remember a statement that says "if you fail to plan you have the plan to fail". You must set your goals on how to be carrying out the duty daily without being compromised. You can set your goals just as the following:

HAVE A PLAN FOR EACH DAY, WEEK, MONTH, AND YEAR

Plan for how you want to spend each day is very important in achieving your purpose. If you don't have a plan you will just get pushed around without having any direction in life. Planning your days will help in reaching your set goals every day in alignment with what matters to you. It is necessary to have a vision and mission statement in your planning. There is no well-designed company without a vision and mission statement which will serve as focus even to a novice in the platform. Your plan will be a basic and focus that is alongside with your vision and mission, and it must be pasted in a place where it must be seen always. Your planning should begin to expand and extend or progress into a weekly plan, monthly plan as you move on you graduates into what we called a long-term plan which is years. This long-term plan will help you when you have started utilizing your potential towards the success of your purpose and people around the world are already feeling your presence through the impact you are making in their lives. With the proper planning, you will know what you ought to achieve in a day, week, month, and year.

Get Machines/Tools

No matter how talented you are you will need an instrument to project your career. If you are gifted in teaching you must have teaching materials like books, chalks, ruler, images, etc. to foster your teaching career. Electronic gadgets are the most instrument teachers are using now. You must be ready to get a computer, a projector with a screen, and many others. If you are an actor or actress, there are some tools you need which include costume for different actions and performances for you to avoid disappointment.

I remember a pianist in the music group who always go out with the rented piano. One day when he has an important outing he was disappointed because people from another group had booked for that same piano which was his own choice. That day I discovered the need for all music instrumentalists to get their instruments. Having your machines or tools at your disposal to be used for the assignment of reaching out to your product to the people at any time you want it, will foster the delivery of your service. In this aspect, human resources management skills will also be employed. Because you cannot rule out the service to be rendered by those around you or working with you. Whether they are properly employed or partially engaged with you to render their service in support of the fulfillment of your purpose they should be properly managed for future performances and avoidance of disappointment. Just like the lover of sports do hire machinery for the achievements of their set goals. There must have been an arrangement and a level of rapport between the machinery and their employers before any outing or performance if a failure will not be entertained.

Get a Good Mentor

Mentorship is a lifespan training. You as a mentee must have a cordial relationship with your mentor through which two of you will always rob mind together on different issues that will benefit you in promoting your purpose. Since you have to know what you are called to do in life and you have got materials tools for articulation and achievement, the next thing for you is to get people of the same mind besides you. I am talking of a visionary mentor, not a vision killer mentor. The importance of this kind of person is because you need a guide when life throws stones at you, you need them to encourage you and get you back on track. Their experienced advice would go along way. Good mentors always counsel and encourage you on how to work harder and move forward towards your set goals. If you set out your goals and your ideas in motion without a good mentor, you are just like a big company without the support of any insurance company, and when the damages occur there will be nothing or nobody to fall back on. Not all the mentors are good. Use all your efforts both physical and spiritual to get the person who has an interest in your talent and set goals as your career mentor.

Organize Yourself

A woman once introduced her husband to me as a man who is not organized. And there was an occasion where her statement was confirmed by the chairman of that occasion. The quality of being organized is known as an organization which is very important to anyone who is to live to his or her maximal potential in life. Being organized cannot be ruled out at all because it deals with arrangements on how to map out your plan. It is necessary even from the beginning of your preparation. The way the program is being strategically structured will show how organized the programmer is. To channel potential towards your purpose, you must be organized. It is very easy to get lost if you are not organized. Take off the unnecessary things to give way for the useful ones. Let your arrangements be intact without any lacunars or vacuum that will create a sense of lapses for the outsiders.

The journey to where we are going is not far, but the place we do branch at are numerous which may eventually not allow us to reach where we planned to go on time.

To reach the peak of our purpose or mission in life is not difficult if we minimize things that do exhaust our potential, and then, channel our potential directly to our purpose.

CHAPTER 4- FULFILLING YOUR PURPOSE WHILE YOU ARE LIVING.

Fulfillment of purpose is a must for anyone that does not want to live a purposeless life and go to the grave with their potential that should be released for great exploitation on earth. So this chapter will focus more on how to utilize your full potential for the fulfillment of your great and discerned on earth. Some people reach this stage of service of fulfillment but fainted right there on the stage, because of a lack of knowledge and capacity for sustainability. It is expedient of you to set your priority toward the achievement of your purpose and to be ready for discharging your potentialat the high level of your capacity. This is a junction in your life that is very crucial and also delicate because, it will bring more profits, high self-esteem, and of course pride will creep in, your ability to be in control is not negotiable. Let us look at some tips for fulfilling the purpose.

I. COMMITTED TO YOUR FULL POTENTIAL

Commitment here is to be sincere and attentive to yourself in fulfilling your divine purpose in life which you have defined. The more you are committed the more you are productive. This commitment involves rehearsal, you continue to do the same thing again and again until you are lust into it, just as to say practice makes perfect.

A. Be focused.

It is very proper for you to be focused on your purpose. I mean your defined purpose through which you are releasing potential. You cannot focus on two things together at the same time or else you lose both of them. Focusing your attention on a particular thing will help you to know the outcome. Your mind must not scatter rather, it must be calm and attentive.

B. Be confident

When talking or discussing your products let self-assurance and feeling of certainty be seen on your face and in your words. if you are not proud of your ability and the product you produced, nobody will patronize you. Confidence must be expressed while carrying out your duty especially in the journey of destiny.

If you lack confidence you are not competent.

C. Be courageous

There are many ways for disappointments to show up. When fearful or nerveless is being entertained in one's life career, failure to produce is inevitable. The spiritless and weak-hearted person will never live to fulfill a destiny or live to utilize potential. Weakness is an agent and instrument the devil is using to downfall people from the height or peak of their purpose.

Your ability to persevere and withstand danger or any form of discouragement will keep you flowing. Encourage and strengthen yourself morally and mentally as a brave and mighty man of valor, no matter the situation and circumstances of life. I want you to know that nobody is out there to make you happy except you. Shun every cowardice and spinelessness spirit, embrace the spirit of fearlessness and courage.

II. FIGHT AGAINST DISTRACTION AROUND YOU

What is a distraction?

How can it affect me?

This was a response of a young man during an employment interview. The truth is that many people had lost their jobs, an uncountable number of people had become disabled while some lost their lives through the motor, train, and airplane accidents because of drivers that pilots the affairs journey entertained distraction while on duties.

Distraction, which is anything or anyone that takes direct or shift one's attention from the primary assignment or from what he or she is doing has caused and made some existing potentials after being utilized became dormant again. This is so devastating!

To be candid, no matter how committed, intelligent, or attentive you are you cannot do without having distraction. Only in your wisdom that you find a way of dealing with it because it comes across everywhere and every profession. To mindfully fight against distraction you will need to pay attention to some of its sources which humans cannot do without having a relationship with.

Distractions Through Friends

Distractions do surface through the people we cherish. When you have something meaningful to do and any of your friends deem it fit to check on you, your friend's visit will take more of your time especially in chatting and cracking jokes. Even when you are not under anybody for supervision, and nobody is waiting for your productivity in the given period; and yet you have a set goal: how are you maintaining your freedom with the entanglement from friends? At this very period of no pressure from anywhere and there is autonomy galore that the discipline should be upheld. It is good to maintain a good relationship with people but it should not be at the detriment of our time scheduled for a purpose. This must be critically looked into for purpose to be fulfilled.

Having a private time when projecting your purpose is needed for a good performance. A musician that suppose to have personal rehearsal in preparation for an important task ahead would fail if he uses rehearsal time to entertain friends. Distractions from the side of friends need to be handled with seriousness and care.

Distractions at your workplace

A workplace is a business place. It is a place where seriousness should be condoned and strictly adhere to. However, the reverse is the case in some places especially among the colleague who is not at the peak of their career. When your seriousness is being noticed your peers may plan and bring disturbance, or confusion to distract your attention from the real thing you are doing. On this, you need to be sensitive and attentive to your duty to achieve the set goals. Any issue in your neighbors' office that does not come to your table and your attention is not invited should be strictly avoided. Most especially during working hours, you should use that available time to think and plan new things along with your purpose.

As a manager or director, eliminating distractions in your workplace is very important. When your desk is surrounded by distractions get up and move yourself to either conference room or nooks where one can quietly work. The expectation of your productivity is very high. Find a way off of being distracted.

Distractions through unplanned events

Just like when you are surf the internet many unwanted and unrequested programs will be popping up on your screen. Such programs were designed just to get your attention from your primary intention. If you click on any of them, they are capable of confusing you and get you lost.

In your schedule, you are to attend to tasks as planned then, another thing you don't arrange in your plan surface with little importance. The right thing is to deal with arranged events first before any other one. The chairman of a meeting who attends to another discussion without being first cleared the list of items in the meeting agenda will be tagged as a failure.

Distraction Through Negative Thoughts

A lot of people missed what God has for them because they entertained negative thoughts in their minds and believe in it. These negative thoughts and fear have dealt with many people by retaining them in a spot of stagnancy and become stinking like unmoved waters. This is exactly what happened to the Israelites in the holy book (Bible) when 12 people were sent to spy the land of their destination (Canaan), 10 out of 12 that were sent entertained negative thoughts with great fear, and they focused their attention on the wrong thing. They looked at the size of the inhabitants of the land rather than the land that God told them to possess. They see all the people there as giants and themselves as grasshoppers (Numbers 13:22-33). Some do look down on themselves and occupy their mind with negative thoughts based on their skin color, lack of education, and social-economic. When will entertain and believe the negative words or ideas that are spoken over us it forms an image on the side of us of who we are and what we can do. That image serves as a ceiling that we cannot rise above. Even though our talents and abilities could take us further we don't allow them to. We need to fight the negativity on the side of us and embrace positive thinking.

Distraction And Time-Waster By Social Media

Many things do distract our attention from what we are doing and waste our time beyond what we can even imagine among which are: Television, Social media, Technology Advancement, etc.

Television for example, if one does not have schedule time for what and the things he does, you can spend half of a day watching one of his favorite channels. There are many people since they are working under the supervision of nobody they became a regular customer to different packages like Nollywood, African Magic, sports, documentaries, etc. Television is one of the distractive tools let me not say the devil is using to waste our time and bring frustration and regression why some important works are there piling up. Time must be set up for everything.

Another aspect is social media, this is a major or most distracted tool affecting many people today. This is concerned with the way we handle the following Facebook, WhatsApp, Twitter, Telegram, Instagram e-mailbox, etc. when there is no allotted time for attending to social media (except on emergency which comes once in a while) there will be a lot of distraction through our gadgets which were not planned for. I have seen a lot of people chatting with friends during working hours for hours abandoned what supposed to be done on time. Social media has caused a distraction and imbalanced in memory and brain performances. The period that the brain ought to rest and refresh and be boosted for another task ahead will be truncated, as a result of mismanagement of time through the handling of social media. We should understand and know that our brain is just like a computer and if you keep using a computer for days without shutting it down or rebooting it, it will start malfunctioning and the results you are expecting will no longer forthcoming because the memory is getting or distracted.

Technology advancement is taken over the world coupled with the use of social media and the way we surf the internet and assessing information globally. This is an era we cannot do without but at the same time we must take caution using them.

III. UNLEASH YOUR POTENTIAL

There are many people outside their, suffering, which your skills of writing, singing, teaching, speaking, acting, counseling, dramatizing, invention, advocate, etc. can solve their problems. The whole world is waiting for the manifestation and presentation of your purpose as the solution to the world's problem. The potential inside of you is useless if you do not talk or tap on it, make use of it for global transformation.

Triggers to unleashing your potential

Believe you can do it

There are people with a mental belief system that nothing good will come from their locality, with that view, they are limiting their capacity of production. To start believing your ability you have to focus on your set goals, trust your capacity that you can achieve those goals within a limited time. Many obstacles and hindrances will arise but all will serve as your stepping stones only when you strongly believe. It will also give you more knowledge and strength.

Develop A Conviction

The sense of conviction you developed about your product will give you audacity and boldness to introduce your products to the consumers in a convincing way that will make them believe what your talent has produced. Consequently, your purpose will be known to the world as the presence of the sun always felt at the sunrise.

Conviction in self reinforces the belief that you are capable of achieving the goals you have set for yourself, that you will be successful despite the hurdles obstacles coming your way, and that you have it in you to stand tall in the face of difficulties. Self-conviction fuels the fire of ambition in you, it makes you feel positive about your ability and makes others believe in you as well.

Maintain Your Positive Imagination

As we use our imagination to conceive new ideas. it is expedient for us to know that there is a negative and positive aspect of imagination. As we cannot get to the office without first getting there in your mind (through imagination). If we see ourselves as a failure within the mind-image. That failure will surely manifest physically in our endeavors. Thus, backward will become the order of the day (God forbid).

Fulfilling a purpose begins with the usefulness of positive imagination. For you not to run dry you must have a bank where you store your imagination as raw materials for future use and dispensation. Imagination and ideas capable of disappearing and evaporating when it is not actualizing and realizing on time. One important thing we must know about every imagination and idea is that it comes for a purpose to transform someone's life and beautify the owner's life. No imagination is to be wasted because God hates a waster and he can never be friends with anyone who is a waster. Once you receive imagination which some people called inspiration you have a new idea to offer which must be handled with proper care.

AVOID A PURPOSELESS LIFE

The word Purposeless is the direct opposite meaning of the word Purpose. Online Dictionary defined purpose as An object to be reached or a target and set goal.

We walk and move around the world to fulfill a purpose. Everything we do is all about the intention to achieve something. We go to school to acquire more knowledge, we learn many things for us to get information and know more about them. That is a great purpose! The purpose is also an intention, a set goal, dreams, and the plan we have in mind to fulfill. Things you do and feel a sense of significance and fulfillment. Contextually, the purpose is the reason and the mission you have on earth to be achieved and fulfilled for the glory of God and the benefits of humanity. Your existence in this world has a reason which you must discover within your capacity and work towards its achievement.

A purposeless life is a life with no future ambition, without dreams, and set goals and it always ends in regret.

When one is aimless, his mind cannot be fixed towards any purpose, he will always be free and idle. To such people, no plan for anything or any day, whatever that comes to their way daily is their plan. They neglect potential and forget their purpose on earth what a purposeless life!

There is ability deposited a man to use and discover is purpose on earth which I called potential. This is inborn ability and enablement that is fueling man's purpose for existence. Failure to utilize it will lead to a purposeless life.

God created us with the ability/potential to be purposeful creative in attempting to the issue in the world and proffer solution.

For us not to live a purposeless life, we need to be asking ourselves the following questions. What is my purpose or mission? What am I created or called to do in life? "

CHAPTER 5- POTENTIALS IN THE GRAVEYARD

One may ask questions such as, why is potential in the graveyard? What is potential doing in the graveyard? How does a potential get to the graveyard? Can potentials come out of the graveyard?

As it is cleared that potential is unrealized ability in form of a gift for transformation in human life, but why potential and not other things in the graveyard which is a place of useless and abandonment. Potential does not exist in a vacuum or isolation but it does in human life. Anywhere humans exist, you see potential also; whether manifesting or not manifesting it would always be there. A graveyard is a place of corpse, human became corpse immediately he or she stopped breathing. At the point a man died, everything in him dies also, but there are many corpses in their life that lived. Unsued gifts and talents become a waste, thus, the potential is buried in the graveyard.

Is there any assignment for potential at the graveyard or any mission to be accomplished by the potential in the graveyard? Ordinarily, the potential in a man is within the scope of his inherent power. It is when utilized and released that the other party would know what you are up to do. Therefore, there is no single assignment for potential at the cemetery or graveyard neither a mission nor work allotted to the potential of a dead person in the cemetery.

When a man is buried, the unused potential of the corpse would be buried as well and become useless because it is inseparable from man. Thus, the potentials lied in the graveyard refers to those good things like unwritten books, yet to be composed of songs, undersigned graphics, unacted drama, unreleased skilled, unfulfilled destinies, etc.

Can potential come out of the graveyard? This is a great question with a direct answer. Potential that exists passively in an unknown place (the mind of Man) has no feather-like bird to act or fly on its own and it cannot be transferred from a dead person to a living person. Of the truth, no problem has ever solved itself without the intervention of man, also no car of different grades can move except man is in control. Everything was created as God wanted it to be, both living and non-living things. Even some living things need the attention of man before it would work or move properly. This shows that nothing in this world is movable without the touch of a man. Inasmuch, as potential is an unrealized ability and a symbol of impact on planet earth; it doesn't mean it lives in isolation but inside of Man.   When anyone dies and gets buried, his potentials dies with him; Potentials of a buried person cannot come out of the cemetery because it is attached to the spirit and the spirit has returned to its Creator. It is a great loss because it is useless!

Potential is an undiscovered and unrealized gift and talent, and thoughts that do surface through imagination as new ideas that are yet to be revealed are capable of transforming into reality. The previous chapters of this book shed more light on how to identify, actualize, and utilize one's potential in life which is of help to anyone who wishes to fulfill the Divine mandate upon his life. Potential in one's life is to be used for its purpose which is to impact the world by influencing and transforming people's life.

There is no one on earth without the potential to do something even though many people are not realizing let alone reaching their potential, they prefer living a normal routine life just like any other person without a focus. One thing you must know is that you are created for a positive change, you are a global transformer. So, rise and use your potential to do something with that your dreams, vision aims, target, objective, and desires now that you are still living.

Andrew Womack in his book titled "Don't limit GOD" said and I quote, *"if you want to go to a place that has the most potential go to the graveyard"*[3] The vast majority of people take their potential to the grave, die without ever realizing their full potential. Hundred of people have dreams and goals that have been set aside because of negative thoughts. Your potential is not meant to be taken to the grave while people that should benefit from it are on earth suffering.

I attended the burial of a man who died at age of 29 without being married. To the knowledge of everyone at his burial service, this man died a premature death; he survived with just his father, mother, and siblings. However, when it comes to the aspects of funeral oration and tribute, I heard different things did by the young man that died at the age of 29 years. Those people who realized their life potentials through this young man from different countries in the world came up and testify to the impact of this young man in their lives. He taught many people how to become witchcraft in handling musical instruments. The studio he worked as an editorial team leader were all surprised by his quick departure. It was then I realized the statement that says "it is not how long but how well". The young man could have died and be buried with his potential and the grave would have robbed him of his potential, if not because he realized his ability and begin to use it for his purpose on time.

Think of your age now what have you done to humanity? What are you doing and what is/are your plan(s) to empty yourself before people bid you farewell to this world and you pass on to the land where potential, talent, gift etc. will be useless (Ecclesiastes . chapter 12 verses 1 to 7)

PROCRASTINATION: AN ENEMY OF POTENTIAL

Postponement is a close friend of regression and procrastination is not only the thief of time but the enemy of potential also because, potential need to be realized, tapped, and use on time. One of the major problems in the journey of success and achievement is procrastination. The language has been I will do it later when I have time, not now. This has pushed many into debt, sent some into prison, and some into the grave. "That sickness that killed Mr. John would not have killed him if to say he acted on a precautionary on time" (said by his brother). There is no enemy or killer of potential than procrastination.

Flourish Joshua, the director of Flourish Joshua Writers and Speakers Academy*(online school)* said in one of his quotes that *"if you continue giving excuses you will be excluded from enjoying divine inheritance, you never know what you are missing by building a mansion in your comfort zone. Breakout and flow with the current of unspeakable sources".* As you continue postponing and procrastinating you are missing the blessing allotted to you at the moment. The day you stepped into this world your time started reading the time you have spent cannot come back again. There was a man in Nigeria that ought to be wedded around January/February 2020 but he postponed the date saying before the year runs out I would reschedule the date because I want to get everything ready. Along the line, a global disease called corona virus (COVID 19), which made the Federal government ban social gathering of any kind until the virus disappear. He was unable to fix the date of the wedding.

One of my lecturers once told us in our final year while giving his words of advice, that anything we need to do in life we must make sure we do it (them) on time. So as not to entertain procrastination at all because of the lessons he had learned through procrastination. He said, he was the best student during his second-degree program (Master degree program at the prestigious University of Ibadan) and almost all of his lecturers called him to come and enroll for his third-degree (Ph.D.) program but he replied that he would find a better time to come. And since then, he has never had that better time because of other responsibilities that keep surrounding him. He concluded is words that no better time will come except we determine to do something at a particular time.

There is a time for everything and a season for every activity and purpose under heaven (Ecclesiastes 3:1). God that created heaven and earth did not postpone any of His works until He accomplished all. Since you are created in the image of God, you don't need to procrastinate what you ought to do now till another time because you don't know what tomorrow will bring, I want you to know that procrastination is the enemy of your destiny. Therefore, oppose it, fight it, and conquer it.

Do not hesitate! Do not negotiate!!Just go for it now!!! Begin and start it now.

DANGER OF UNUSED POTENTIAL

It is going to be a very big disaster when you leave this world for others and you are asked by your Creator that you did not use your potential to do what He created you to do or what He asked you to do in the world. I am convinced that if people know the mistake they were making in not using their potential they would think twice. Unused potential can harm your purpose of living, if there is one thing that grief God about man, it is not using his potential. The level of poverty we have in this country "Nigeria" (apart from mismanagement of resources) is a result of unused potential that is rampant. Proverbs from the Holy Scripture says: "Diligent hands will rule but, laziness ends in forced labor" (Proverbs 12:24)you are created with potential that can be a benefit to others. It would be dangerous for you not to use your potential judiciously because those that are to benefit from the outcome of your potential will be reinforced course on you through their Spirit (in the spiritual realm)

DO NOT BE UNFRUITFUL

Unfruitfulness is the same thing with barrenness, on a normal circumstance no couple would be joined together after some years without a child and be happy. The thoughts of people about their family will not be friendly because they will be expecting them to have started reproducing. An Engineer who was sponsored in school by a well-wisher will lose his dignity in the sight of his benefactor that responsible for his training financially if he refuses to go to the field for reproduction (practicing). Likewise, everyone that gave birth to a child will equally like his or her child to reproduce and keep the chain moving. The same way of expectation is God having from us because he has deposited the ability and capacity in us to carry out the assignments.

The story of the unfruitful fig tree in the Scripture is a big challenge and example for us. The fig tree was very leafy and Jesus went there to eat fruit from it but, alas! There was no fruit. He (Jesus) then cursed the fig tree that why should it be expanding and leafy without fruit. The following day the fig tree in question has withered. (Matthew 21:17 to 19). Your potential is given to you for productivity and for helping people around the world. The unproductive potential will lead to dryness and punishment by the creator and the giver of potential. (God).

The life of an ungrateful servant in the Bible is another great lesson for us in this aspect. Who was given a potential talent to trade with but buried it without utilizing it for any profit? When his Master returned, having been told about the story, he took the talent from him and commanded that he should be carried into the lake of fire. The unused potential is dangerous because it can work against us even after leaving this planet Earth therefore, strive and struggle to reach your full potential.

LIVE TO YOUR FULL POTENTIAL

Your potential is to be a source of pleasure and satisfaction to you in life. Our Creator gives us the potential to serve as a conduit to having our joy fulfill as we work on our purpose. However, there is an adage that says: "a river that forgets its source will eventually dry up" any human being that forgets or partially forget his or her source (God) will finally end up unproductive in life. (Not reproduction on giving birth) but in the area of fulfilling the destiny because, when God was to create human being He spoke to Himself in Trinitarian form He molded the man, breathe His breath into man's nostrils and He gave man freedom of choice. Now take the man out of God, he dies. Many people because of freedom of choice have deviated from their source who is God. Thus, the assurance of surviving is no more there. Not for surviving sake but surviving in fulfilling their purpose through the potentials that God has deposited in their life. This has caused many people to live a figurehead life. (Life without impartation).

Those that get it right early enough are now on top. I know it is not easy for a beginner. But, start somewhere now. Living up to your fullest potential will not happen in one day nether will it happen by accident, it would only happen over some time, only after you decide to come out of your comfort zone and take action to utilize it, knowing what you are good at and what you want to do in life we make your life more satisfying and fulfilling.

CONCLUSION

Potential in one's life makes a way for him and distinguishes him among others when utilized properly. The joy is that no one on earth is without potential that will make him great. It is also the joy of originator and giver of potential to see Man utilizing his potential for a great impartation. No matter the color of your skin, lack of education, or socioeconomic status, you still have the potential to use in fulfilling your purpose of existence.

Some were not aware of this till they died and left this planet Earth, some were aware but they took the issue of potential lightly and nonchalantly. Many keep on postponing and procrastinating until death removes them from this planet Earth.

The truth is that no potential is to be useful in the graveyard where you are going after leaving this world/ planet Earth. It is advisable for you after reading through this book to take a step toward realizing and releasing your potential for great impartation through the purpose you have discovered.

Your action this time around will go a long way. Mind you, the journey of potential cannot be fulfilled when you leave the source of potential and destiny behind who is God Almighty, Cleave to Him today and your potential will be realized and utilized.

---

[1]Merriam-Webster dictionary online, https://www.merriam-webster.com
[2]Online English dictionary, https://trovami.altervista.org
[3]Andrew Womack, Don't Limit God, (Harrison House Tulsa Ok, 2014), p. 57.

ACKNOWLEDGEMENT

All thanks to the Almighty God for inspiring me to write this book and the grace to pursue His purpose for my life.

I appreciate my lord Bishop, The Right Reverend I. K. Tasie, the Bishop, Diocese of Ngbo. For his support materially, spiritually, and also foreword of this book.

And my home Bishop, Right Reverend Andrew, The Bishop Diocese of Ketu.

I cannot forget to acknowledge the right Reverend Williams O. Fasina, The Bishop, Diocese of Ijesa North

I thank my Presbyter also The Very Reverend E. E. Okwor for his support and writing a foreword of this book, and all the ministers in the Diocese of Ngbo.

Special thanks to Pastor Ife Adetona, President, Sons, and Daughters of Zion Worldwide for reading through this book and suggested some corrections and observations, and for writing a foreword of this book.

I appreciate my father who brought me up in the ministry; the Very Reverend J. Ade Abiodun. He is currently the principal of Methodist Comprehensive High School(Mission).

My Home Cathedral Presbyter, The Very Reverend J. B. Osunrotimi, and all the ministers of the gospel in the Diocese of Ketu for their prayers.

My unreserved thanks go to my lecturers in both seminaries for their impartations, time will not permit me to mention all their names, but I will mention a few. The Very Reverend J. O. Ayodele, my tutorial master and SUBDEAN elect of Immanuel College of Theology and Christian Education Ibadan,

The Very Reverend Dr. R.

 A. Idialu the RECTOR elect of Methodist Theological Institute Sagamu, The Very Reverend Dr. E. A. Adetunji who is now in Wesley University Ondo, The Very Reverend A. O. Kuyebi who is now in Hoare's Memorial Methodist Cathedral, Yaba.

I am particularly indebted to my parents, my father, and my mother for their tireless efforts, 'isu omo ajina fun yin je o'.

Finally, I appreciate my one and only "Queen" Adefunke, and my daughter for their support and encouragement; they have been there through the journey to completing this project.

I must not forget to thank the entire team members of Flourish Joshua Writers and Speakers Academy for making this book a reality within a short period.

ABOUT THE AUTHOR

Rev. Jonah Sunday Morenikeji

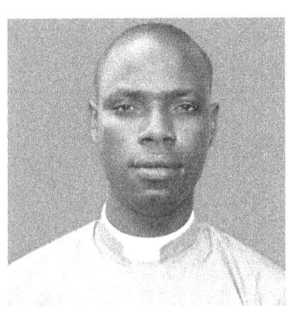

Rev. Jonah Sunday. Morenikeji is a certified writer and public speaker, is a minister of God in Methodist Church Nigeria, currently serving in the Diocese of Ngbo, Ebonyi State, Nigeria.

He is a graduate of Immanuel College of Theology and Christian Education Ibadan and Methodist Theological Institute Sagamu respectively. He obtained the following certificates: DIP. RS. (University of Ibadan), B. TH. (ICTACE), CCL and CWS (MTIS). He is from Imeko, Ogun State, Nigeria: married, and the marriage is blessed with children.

UNTITLED

AFTERWORD

Potentials in your life are like mineral resources if not tapped upon for years, it will not work on its own till you die and be buried with it. You have been hearing and seeing people that lived and living to their full potentials in life. But the secret of their achievements somehow unknown. Not that they have no challenges in life. Not that they were/are supernatural beings. But they discovered the purpose of their lives and used their potentials towards it. This book exposed some tips for living the fullest potential for the manifestation of the purpose. Your potentials are not useful in the grave. Get a copy of this book, read and digest it, and begin to experience transformation.